D0382688

ZOOM IN ON
FIREFLIES

Melissa Stewart

Enslow Elementary

CONTENTS

WORDS TO KNOW

antennae (an TEN ee)— Two long, thin body parts on the head of insects and some other animals. Antennae help animals sense the world around them.

lantern (LAN tern)—The part of a firefly's body that gives off light. It is in the abdomen.

larva (LAHR vuh)—The second part in the life cycle of some insects. A larva changes into a pupa.

nectar (NEK tuhr)—A sugary liquid that many flowers make. Some fireflies drink it.

pupa (PYOO puh)—The third part in the life cycle of some insects. A pupa changes into an adult.

FIREFLY HOMES

ZOOM BUBBLE

Fireflies live in many parts of the world. In some places, people call them lightning bugs.

These insects like warm, damp places away from lights. You can find them near ponds and streams. Look for them in fields and backyards, too.

PARTS OF A FIREFLY

antenna

head

thorax

wing

eye

lantern

leg

abdomen

FIREFLY BODY

ZOOM BUBBLE

A firefly is not a fly. It belongs to a group of insects called beetles. It has six legs. And its body has three parts. They are the head, the thorax, and the abdomen.

FIREFLY FLASH

Fireflies are famous for their flash. Why do they glow? They rest during the day and come out at night. They use the **lantern** on their back end to find mates in the dark.

FIREFLY LEGS

ZOOM BUBBLE

A firefly has six legs. They are attached to the middle of its body.

Female fireflies spend most of their time on the ground. They use their legs to walk from place to place. Males spend much more time flying.

FIREFLY WINGS

ZOOM BUBBLE

Most fireflies have two sets of wings. The front wings protect the back wings. When a firefly is ready to fly, it lifts the front wings. Then it spreads the back wings and takes off. The back wings flap through the air.

This female firefly is flashing
its lantern in the grass.

FIREFLY EYES

ZOOM BUBBLE

A firefly has two huge eyes. They can see right and left, up and down— all at the same time.

A male firefly needs to see well. He uses his eyes to spot flashing females in the grass.

FIREFLY ANTENNAE

ZOOM BUBBLE

A firefly has two long antennae on its head. Some are straight. Others are feathery. But they all do the same things. They can feel and hear and smell.

17

FIREFLY FOOD

ZOOM BUBBLE

Most adult fireflies do not eat at all. They live on fat stored in their bodies.

Some fireflies sip sweet, sugary nectar from plants. A few eat other kinds of insects.

FIREFLY GLOWWORMS

When a firefly comes out of its egg, it looks like a worm. It gives off a soft light.

The glowworm hunts slugs, worms, and snails. It eats and grows for up to two years. Then it becomes a pupa.

LIFE CYCLE

A firefly begins life inside an EGG.

A firefly LARVA is called a glowworm.

ADULT fireflies live just a few days. Most of them don't eat at all.

On the outside, a PUPA stays still. But its body is changing inside.

LEARN MORE

BOOKS

Ashley, Susan. *Incredible Fireflies.* Milwaukee: Gareth Stevens, 2011.

Hudak, Heather C., ed. *Fireflies.* New York: Weigl Publishers, 2009.

Miller, Connie Colwell. *Fireflies.* Mankato, Minn.: Capstone Press, 2005.

Rau, Dana Meachen. *Flash, Firefly, Flash!* New York: Marshall Cavendish Benchmark, 2008.

WEB SITES

National Geographic. *Firefly.*
  <http://animals.nationalgeographic.com/animals/bugs/firefly>

Ready, Set, Glow! *Activity Sheets.*
  <http://readysetglow.org/activitysheets/index.html>

INDEX

Enslow Elementary, an imprint of Enslow Publishers, Inc.
Enslow Elementary® is a registered trademark of Enslow
Publishers, Inc.

Copyright © 2014 by Melissa Stewart

Library of Congress Cataloging-in-Publication Data

Stewart, Melissa.
  Zoom in on fireflies / Melissa Stewart.
    p. cm. — (Zoom in on insects!)
  Summary: "Provides information for readers about a
firefly's home, food, and body"—Provided by publisher.
  Includes index.
  ISBN 978-0-7660-4213-1
  1. Fireflies—Juvenile literature. I. Title. II. Series: Stewart,
Melissa. Zoom in on insects.
  QL596.L28S74 2014
  595.7644—dc23

                                        2012040389

Future editions:
Paperback ISBN: 978-1-4644-0369-9
EPUB ISBN: 978-1-4645-1204-9
Single-User PDF ISBN: 978-1-4646-1204-6
Multi-User PDF ISBN: 978-0-7660-5836-1

Printed in the United States of America

112013 Lake Book Manufacturing, Inc. Melrose Park, IL

10 9 8 7 6 5 4 3 2 1

Series Literacy Consultant:
Allan A. De Fina, PhD
Past President of the New Jersey Reading Association
Chairperson, Department of Literacy Education
New Jersey City University
Jersey City, New Jersey

Photo Credits: David Cappaert, Michigan State University,
Bugwood.org, pp. 10, 11; © James E. Lloyd/Animals Animals,
p. 18; Kazuo Unno/Nature Production/Minden Pictures, p. 22
(bottom right); © Dwight Kuhn, pp. 1, 4, 6, 9, 12, 15, 16, 19, 20,
22 (top left, top right); © David Kuhn/Dwight Kuhn Photography,
p. 13; Mitsuhiko Imamori/Minden Pictures, p. 8; Satoshi
Kuribayashi/Nature Production/Minden Pictures, pp. 21, 22
(bottom left); Shane Cummins/Photos.com, p. 17; Shutterstock.
com, p. 2, 3, 7; Stephen Dalton/Minden Pictures, p. 14; Tyler
Fox/Photos.com, p. 5.

Cover Photo: © Dwight Kuhn

Enslow Elementary
an imprint of
Enslow Publishers, Inc.
40 Industrial Road
Box 398
Berkeley Heights, NJ 07922
USA
http://www.enslow.com

Science Consultant:
Helen Hess, PhD
Professor of Biology
College of the Atlantic
Bar Harbor, Maine